YOU CHOOSE™
BOOKS

BUILDING THE
TRANSCONTINENTAL
RAILROAD

An Interactive Engineering Adventure

by Steven Otfinoski

Consultant:
Malcolm J. Rohrbough, PhD
Professor Emeritus, Department of History
The University of Iowa

CAPSTONE PRESS
a capstone imprint

You Choose Books are published by Capstone Press,
1710 Roe Crest Drive, North Mankato, Minnesota 56003
www.capstonepub.com

Library of Congress Cataloging-in-Publication Data
Otfinoski, Steven, author.
  The building of the transcontinental railroad : an interactive engineering adventure / by Steven
Otfinoski.
      pages cm.—(You choose. Engineering marvels)
  Summary:"Explores various perspectives on the process of building the transcontinental railroad.
The reader's choices reveal the historical details"—Provided by publisher.
  Audience: Ages 8–12.
  Audience: Grades 4 to 6.
  Includes bibliographical references and index.
  ISBN 978-1-4914-0401-0 (library binding)
  ISBN 978-1-4914-0406-5 (paperback)
  ISBN 978-1-4914-0410-2 (ebook PDF)
1. Railroads—United States—History—19th century—Juvenile literature. 2. Pacific railroads—
Juvenile literature. I. Title.
  TF23.O84 2015
  385.0973—dc23   2013047701

Editorial Credits
Adrian Vigliano, editor; Veronica Scott, designer; Wanda Winch, media researcher; Laura Manthe,
production specialist

Photo Credits
The Bridgeman Art Library: Kenneth John Petts, 83; Capstone, 6; Corbis, 62, Bettmann, 39;
Courtesy of the Chinese Historical Society of America (CHSA), artist Jake Lee, 12; CriaImages:
Jay Robert Nash Collection, cover (all), 100; The Denver Public Library, 56; Getty Images Inc:
Hulton Archive, 50, PhotoQuest, 76, Underwood Archives, 26; Library of Congress: Prints and
Photographs Division, 10, 17, 20, 40, 67, 88; National Archives and Records Administration,
94; North Wind Picture Archives, 102, 104; The Powder Monkeys, Cape Horn, 1865, ©Mian
Situ, licensed by The Greenwich Workshop, Inc. www.greenwichworkshop.com, 37; Shutterstock:
alekup, grunge blueprint design, Sociologas, graph paper design; Ten Miles in One Day, Victory
Camp, Utah, April 28, 1869, ©Mian Situ, licensed by The Greenwich Workshop, Inc. www.
greenwichworkshop.com, 81, Yale Collection of American Literature, Beinecke Rare Book and
Manuscript Library, 46, 70

Printed in Canada.
032014   008086FRF14

TABLE OF CONTENTS

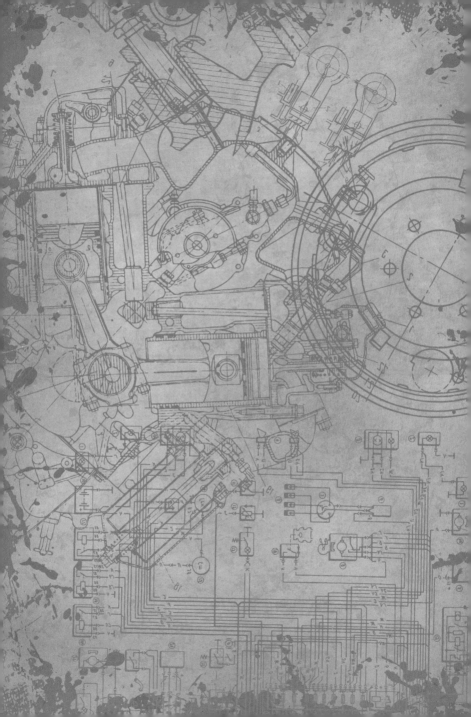

ABOUT YOUR ADVENTURE

YOU live in a nation on the move in the 1860s. The U.S. government gives two railroad companies the job of building the first transcontinental railroad. This railroad will allow people to travel west more quickly to start new lives and pursue new opportunities.

In this book, you'll explore how the choices people made meant the difference between life and death. The events you'll experience happened to real people.

Chapter One sets the scene. Then you choose which path to read. Follow the directions at the bottom of each page. The choices you make will change your outcome. After you finish one path, go back and read the others for new perspectives and more adventures.

YOU CHOOSE the path
you take through history.

The transcontinental railroad was planned to run across the United States from east to west. Before this project, railroad tracks only reached as far west as Omaha, Nebraska.

CHAPTER 1

FROM COAST TO COAST

It is July 1, 1862, a historic day in American history. President Abraham Lincoln has just signed the Pacific Railroad Act. It will assign two private railroad companies the job of completing 1,775 miles of railroad across the United States. Such a transcontinental railroad has been the dream of many Americans for years.

The first American-made steam locomotive to run on a commercial railroad line was the *Tom Thumb* in 1830. Over the next 20 years more than 9,000 miles of railroad tracks crossed the eastern United States. But none have gone farther west than the inland towns along the Missouri River.

When gold was discovered in California in 1848, thousands of people left their homes in the eastern United States and headed west. The most common route was a dangerous overland journey by wagon train.

A second route was a difficult six-month voyage by ship from the East Coast down around South America's Cape Horn and then up the Pacific Ocean to California.

A final route consisted of taking a ship across the Gulf of Mexico and then crossing the Isthmus of Panama, a thin strip of land, to the Pacific. Those who got through Panama without dying of a tropical disease could then board a ship for California.

A transcontinental railroad would make the overland journey to California far safer and quicker than any of these options.

In 1862 two companies were given the job of building the railroad—the Central Pacific and the Union Pacific. The Union Pacific would build track west from Omaha, Nebraska, along the Missouri River. The Central Pacific would lay track eastward from Sacramento, California. At some point the two railroads would meet up and the line would be completed.

Both railroads were run by ambitious, powerful men. The Central Pacific was owned by California businessmen Collis Huntington, Charles Crocker, Leland Stanford, and Mark Hopkins. Stanford was elected governor of California in 1861, only months after the railroad was incorporated. They became known as "The Big Four." The Union Pacific was headed by Dr. Thomas Durant, who was more concerned with making money than providing a transportation line for the country.

Turn the page.

The Central Pacific employed mostly Chinese immigrants. These workers had the challenging task of building trestles and bridges across the towering Sierra Nevada, a mountain range that begins just 50 miles east of Sacramento. In some cases they had to blast the granite rock of the mountains to create tunnels and roadbeds for the railroad.

Peter Cooper built the small *Tom Thumb* locomotive to convince railroad owners to begin using steam engines. The owners were impressed and steam locomotion became common on railroads.

The Union Pacific hired many Irishmen—some American-born and some immigrants. Their path lay mostly across the flat lands of the Great Plains. Along the way they would encounter many dangers—hostile American Indians, blinding snowstorms, and powerful rainstorms.

The ongoing Civil War (1861-1865) fought between the Northern and Southern states, as well as financial problems, slowed progress initially for both railroads. However, by 1864, the Central Pacific and Union Pacific were forging ahead.

You are needed to help build the railroad that will span the nation. Which railroad will you work for? And what job will you take on?

To become a Chinese worker for the Central Pacific, turn to page 13.

To work as an Irish laborer for the Union Pacific, turn to page 41.

To serve as an engineer for the Central Pacific in the final race to complete the railroad, turn to page 71.

Chinese laborers did some of the most dangerous work in the transcontinental railroad project.

CHAPTER 2

A PATH THROUGH THE MOUNTAINS

It is October 1865. The Civil War ended just six months earlier, and the government seeks to unify the country by building a transcontinental railroad.

You are a young Chinese immigrant. You arrived in San Francisco by ship only a few years ago. You tried your luck mining for gold, but like most fortune seekers, you didn't strike it rich. Now you are living with your cousin Li and his family in San Francisco's busy Chinatown. Li has just found work with the Central Pacific Railroad, building the railroad line from Sacramento eastward. Li wants you to join him working for the railroad.

Turn the page.

"Thousands of Chinese are already laying tracks for the railroad," Li tells you. "It's hard work, but the pay is good—$30 a month."

You've never been afraid of hard work, and you agree to go with Li. Together you head southeast for the Sierra Nevada, where the Central Pacific is laying track.

You arrive at a place called Dutch Flat, deep in the mountains. Bridges and trestles have been built to cross from mountain to mountain. But the difficult landscape slows down the work, and the hardest part is still to come. You look up at a 2,000-foot-high cliff of granite. "How will the railroad ever get over that mountain?" you ask Li.

"It won't get over it," says a tall, sturdy white man overhearing your conversation. "It'll go around it."

The man who spoke introduces himself as your new boss, James Strobridge. You've heard he's a tough leader, but he respects his workers.

"Boys, welcome to Cape Horn," Strobridge says. "We call her Cape Horn because she's a devil to get around just like the tip of South America. We're cutting into her side far enough to run the tracks around her."

Strobridge explains that you have three work options. You can chisel the cliff face in a basket. You can lower and lift the baskets the chiselers ride in by ropes. Or you can remain on the ground, filling in a ravine the tracks must cross.

15

To work in the baskets on the cliff side, turn to page 16.
To work lowering and raising the baskets, turn to page 17.
To work filling in the ravine, turn to page 23.

You and Li are taken to the top of Cape Horn, where a large woven basket is waiting for you. This is the same kind of basket workers in China use to work in the mountains. A workman hands you your tools—a hand drill, a hammer, matches, and a small keg of black gunpowder. You knew the railroad work would be hard, but you didn't know it would be this dangerous. You and Li climb into the basket as two other Chinese workers handle the ropes that lower it down the cliff side.

You notice a painted dragon on the side of the basket. It is a symbol of good luck. You decide you will need plenty of luck for this job.

Turn to page 18.

The ropes on the basket are attached to pulleys. You are responsible for lowering and then raising the men who work in them. The job takes plenty of muscle and concentration.

As you begin to lower a basket, a bee lands on your arm. You want to swat it, but you're holding the rope with both hands. What if the bee stings you? You might lose the rope entirely. You could swat it with one hand easily.

A Chinese railroad worker stands at the entrance to a tunnel in the Sierra Nevada.

17

To risk getting stung, turn to page 19.

To swat the bee, turn to page 33.

Inch by inch, you descend the side of the granite cliff. You look down and see men far below: they appear to be the size of ants.

The basket halts and shakes slightly. A shiver of fear runs down your spine. "Let's get to work," says Li. You chip away at the hard rock with your drill and hammer. Soon you have carved out holes big enough to put in a good amount of the black gunpowder.

Li signals you to light the fuse to set off the powder. You have been told to light the fuse and then tug on the rope to signal the men above to heave you up. But will you have enough time to escape the blast? Maybe you should tug on the rope first and light the fuse as you are lifted.

To light the fuse first, turn to page 20.

To tug on the rope first, turn to page 36.

You do your best to ignore the bee. To your relief, it crawls down your arm and flies away. With the basket lowered to its proper location, you and Li make the pulley secure. You have a short break before another pair of workers needs to be hauled up. The work is hard and soon you are covered in sweat. By the end of the day, your muscles are aching.

You and Li and the other Chinese men eat a dinner of cuttlefish, white rice, and fresh vegetables. You and the other Chinese workers have to provide your own meals, and this exotic food has to be shipped in from San Francisco. But it's worth the cost to have healthful, familiar foods to eat.

19

Turn to page 22.

You'd better follow orders. You light the fuse. Li tugs on the rope. You watch the fuse burn as the basket begins to rise. You close your eyes, afraid to look. Suddenly a loud explosion rocks the basket. You look down and see smoke rising from the cliff face. You've survived your first assignment.

The basket reaches the top and you climb out. One of the rope pullers slaps you on the back. "Good work!" he says. Your legs feel a bit shaky but you manage a laugh.

A group of Chinese workers take a break from excavating the Central Pacific's track bed in 1867.

You do two more runs. Then it's time to take a break. You and Li join a circle of other Chinese workers sitting around a small fire and a boiling kettle. As someone hands you a cup of hot tea, you notice a stocky white man with a black beard standing nearby. "Lookee there," he says to his friends. "The Chinamen are drinking their hot water."

Suddenly the bearded man reaches out and pulls on Li's hair, which is braided in a traditional queue ponytail. Li falls back and spills his tea. The man laughs.

You get up, furious.

"Well, this one thinks he's a man!" the bearded fellow cries, walking toward you.

Li whispers to you, "Forget it. I'm all right."

To ignore the bully, turn to page 27.

To stand up to the bully, turn to page 29.

"Maybe we should volunteer for another job," you say to your cousin as you eat.

"Like what? Going down the cliff in one of those baskets? Not for me," Li says.

"We could work in the ravine dumping dirt and rock," you reply. "At least we'll get to move around and see something. It's boring up on that mountaintop."

Li considers this for a moment and then shakes his head. "No, I think I'll stay where I am. You should too."

But you've already made your decision.

Go to page 23.

The ravine is an enormous gash in the earth between the mountains. Dozens of workers are pushing wheelbarrows of dirt and rock and dumping it into the ravine. You join them. You feel it will take months to fill the hole. After a few hours, your back is aching from shoveling the earth into the wheelbarrow. Your arms ache too from pushing the heavy wheelbarrow across the rocky terrain to the ravine. You begin to wonder whether you made the right choice of work.

You notice some men are driving horses that are pulling carts to the ravine. This seems like an easier way of moving the rubble and dirt. Maybe you can convince one of the workers to trade a horse cart for a wheelbarrow.

To stick with your wheelbarrow, turn to page 24.
To try to switch to a horse cart, turn to page 25.

You decide to stick with your trusty wheelbarrow. As you are unloading a load of earth and rock from another wheelbarrow, an older Chinese worker approaches you.

"You work hard, my son," he says. "The American workers don't work so hard and yet they get $10 more pay each month than we Chinese do."

You didn't know that, but it doesn't surprise you.

"A group of us are going on strike," the man continues. "We demand $40 a month and a shorter workday. Will you join us?"

You would like better pay and a shorter workday, but you also don't want to lose your job. The older man waits patiently for your answer.

To join the strikers, turn to page 34.

To stay on the job, turn to page 26.

You approach a tired looking Chinese worker leading a horse with a cart near the edge of the ravine.

"Would you want to trade your cart for this wheelbarrow?" you ask him.

He surprises you by immediately agreeing to the trade. As he rolls your wheelbarrow back for more dirt, he says, "But I'd better warn you—that horse has a mind of its own."

The man is right. The horse is as stubborn as a mule. You move slowly, trying to lead the horse down a path running along the edge of the ravine. Suddenly the horse stops dead and refuses to move forward.

25

You pull but the horse won't budge. You move around behind the horse, trying to think of a new way to approach the problem. Nervously you eye the steep drop next to the cart. Suddenly the horse kicks its back legs, nearly hitting you.

Turn to page 35.

You politely refuse to join the strike. Before he can argue, you go back to work.

Later in the day, you notice a large man watching you work. He approaches and you suddenly recognize him. He's Charles Crocker, general superintendent for the Central Pacific and one of its four owners.

"Son, I've had my eye on you. You're a hard worker and you seem intelligent," he says. "I need men like you. I'm going to give you a promotion."

26

Chinese laborers used horses and carts in their work to build solid paths through the Sierra Nevada.

Turn to page 32.

Li is right. It's not worth getting into trouble over this bully. You sit down again.

"What's the matter, Chinaman?" cries the bearded bully. "Are you turning yellow?"

"That's enough!" cries James Strobridge, rushing over. "Get back to work, O'Neill, and leave the celestials alone. They do their work just fine."

O'Neill and his friends mutter to themselves. But they don't dare talk back to Strobridge.

"What did he call us?" you ask Li.

"Celestials," he replies. "It's because we come from China—the Celestial Kingdom."

Several months pass, and the work on Cape Horn is at an end. You and Li are now assigned to work in one of the 12 tunnels that need to be dug through the mountains.

Turn to page 28.

"You'll be working with a new explosive, five times more powerful than gunpowder," Strobridge explains. "It's called nitroglycerine and it's highly unstable. Disturb it in any way, and it'll blow you to kingdom come."

You and Li head into the tunnel, handling the nitro as if it were a sleeping baby. You use your drill and hammer to make a hole to insert the nitro inside the tunnel wall.

"It's big enough," Li says. He wants to get the first blast with the nitro over as quickly as possible.

You don't agree. You think the hole needs to be a bit deeper so the bottle of nitro doesn't fall out and kill you and everyone else in the tunnel.

28

To continue to drill, turn to page 37.

To stop drilling, turn to page 30.

"Why don't you pick on someone your own size?" you say to the bearded man.

He flashes a cruel grin. "You mean someone like you?" he says.

Li tugs at your leg, urging you to stop, but you ignore him. "That's right," you say boldly.

"Come on," says the bully. "Let's see how a Chinaman fights."

He steps in and takes a swing at your chest. You dodge the blow and the man falls down. As he gets up, you punch him in the mouth. He wipes some blood from his lips. His eyes flash with fury, and he pulls a Bowie knife from his boot.

You gulp as you see the long blade. Maybe it would be best to try to end the fight peacefully. Then you notice a crowbar close by on the ground.

To go for the crowbar, turn to page 31.

To try to end the fight peacefully, turn to page 38.

You agree to see whether the vial of nitro fits into the hole before you drill again. It just fits. Li lights the fuse, and you and the other workers rush back to the front of the tunnel. Seconds pass. Then there is a tremendous explosion.

When the dust settles, you head back into the tunnel. The nitro has turned 10 feet of rock to rubble.

"I guess Mr. Strobridge was right," you say. "This nitro is powerful stuff."

In the days ahead, you continue to blast through the mountain rock until the tunnel is complete. Now it's time for other workers to lay track through it.

Your leadership role in the tunnel has gotten the attention of Strobridge and his boss, Charles Crocker, co-owner and general superintendent for the railroad.

Turn to page 32.

You reach down and grab the crowbar. The bearded man comes at you with his knife. You strike, knocking the knife out of his hand.

At that moment James Strobridge comes along. He sees the crowbar and tells you to drop it.

"I won't tolerate fighting on the job," he says.

Li tries to tell the boss that you were only defending yourself, but Strobridge doesn't listen. "You're fired," he tells you. "And so are you, O'Neill," he says to the bearded man. "Go pick up your pay at the office."

Now you must make the journey back to San Francisco and hope you can find another job. Whatever it is, it won't be as exciting as working for the Central Pacific.

THE END

To follow another path, turn to page 11.
To read the conclusion, turn to page 101.

Crocker makes you a foreman for a gang of 12 Chinese workers. You take your job seriously and so do the men working under you. You set a new record for tracks laid in one day. The record becomes the envy of every other work team.

At last you get through the mountains that have taken so long to conquer. The land is flat and you lay more track with each day that passes. But there are still many miles of track to go before the Central Pacific meets up with the Union Pacific. You plan to be there for the last mile, when the two railroads meet and the job of building the first transcontinental railroad is finished.

32

THE END

To follow another path, turn to page 11.
To read the conclusion, turn to page 101.

You swat the bee, letting go of the rope with your right hand. You got it! But then you hear a scream below. You look at Li. Both of you are stunned.

In the moment that you took your hand off the rope, the basket jerked, and one of the workers in it fell out. You hear his cry as he falls over a thousand feet to his death far below. It is a sound you will carry with you for the rest of your life. Through your own carelessness you have brought about the death of one of your countrymen. After a few days you quit your job on the railroad, having decided to look for safer work in San Francisco.

33

THE END

To follow another path, turn to page 11.
To read the conclusion, turn to page 101.

You join the strike. Unfortunately, the Central Pacific refuses to meet your demands. There aren't enough of you to make the strike effective. You think you'll lose your job, but Strobridge is desperate to get through the mountains and needs every man.

By now, you have been working for the railroad for nearly two years. You feel like an old hand. Someday you will be able to tell your grandchildren that you helped build the first transcontinental railroad.

THE END

To follow another path, turn to page 11.
To read the conclusion, turn to page 101.

You jump back from the horse just in time to avoid being kicked. As you land you lose your balance and tumble into the ravine. It's a long fall to the rocky bottom. You are alive, but your left leg is in terrible pain.

Workers rush to your aid. They carry you out of the ravine on a long wooden plank. You are taken to a makeshift hospital where a doctor pronounces your leg broken in three places. The railroad will move on, but you won't go with it.

THE END

To follow another path, turn to page 11.
To read the conclusion, turn to page 101.

You decide to take no chances in getting blown up. You tug on the rope. Before you can strike the match, the basket jerks upward. The rope men are doing their job—only too well for your liking. A few minutes later, you are at the mountaintop. As you climb out of the basket, Strobridge approaches you.

"Why didn't I hear the explosion?" he asks you.

You explain you didn't have time to light the fuse.

"You didn't follow orders," says Strobridge.

"We'll do it right the next time," says Li quickly.

"There won't be a next time for you two," says Strobridge. "You're fired."

So ends your job on the transcontinental railroad.

THE END

To follow another path, turn to page 11.
To read the conclusion, turn to page 101.

You drill a little deeper. Sparks fly as you pound the drill with your hammer. You watch in horror as one spark lands on the vial of nitro. The explosion is deafening, but you don't hear it. You are killed instantly, along with the other workers in the tunnel. This tragic accident will stop the Central Pacific from using nitroglycerine again. That's a good thing, but unfortunately it's too late for you.

Drill-and-hammer teams used explosives to blast through the mountains. This was some of the most dangerous work on the railroad.

THE END

To follow another path, turn to page 11.
To read the conclusion, turn to page 101.

You step away and turn your back on your enemy. You don't think the man would stab you in the back. He doesn't, but calls you a coward. You don't like hearing that, but you see no sense in continuing the fight. This job is too important to you. You and Li return to work. Although you occasionally see the bully and his friends, there are no more confrontations. You think maybe Strobridge talked to them about leaving you and the other Chinese workers alone.

Months pass and Cape Horn is finally conquered. The digging and blasting you have done has made a roadbed around the cliff that rises like a climbing snake.

One job is done, but plenty of work lies ahead. Tunnels must be dug through the mountains, and winter is coming.

You and Li have proved yourselves on the mountain. You have confidence that you can meet the challenges ahead. America is still a new land to you, but you feel a part of it now. You have left your mark on the railroad that will unite this nation. And you take great pride in that.

By the time the transcontinental railroad was finished, the Central Pacific had employed more than 12,000 Chinese workers.

THE END

To follow another path, turn to page 11.
To read the conclusion, turn to page 101.

A track gang works along one of the many long, flat stretches of the railroad.

CHAPTER 3

CROSSING THE GREAT PLAINS

It is June 1867. You are a young Irishman and a veteran of the recent Civil War. You proudly fought on the Union side. But when the war ended in April 1865, jobs were scarce for soldiers returning to civilian life. You headed west looking for work and new opportunities. You took every job you could get, but these opportunities rarely lasted more than a few days or weeks.

Then you heard the Union Pacific was hiring more men to build the railroad west from Nebraska. It is one of two companies building a railroad that will span the country.

Turn the page.

The Union Pacific started from Omaha, Nebraska, the place where the eastern rails built so far had ended. Since then, it has crossed the state of Nebraska, laying more than 300 miles of track. You and other job seekers apply at the main office. Hiring is done by the chief engineer, Grenville Dodge. Dodge was a Union Army general who fought bravely in the Civil War and was seriously wounded.

When Dodge learns you are a war veteran, he takes a personal interest in you.

"As a fellow Union man, I'm going to give you a choice of jobs on the Union Pacific," the general says.

"You can move on to Julesburg, where the railroad camp is currently located, and go to work laying track. Or you can choose to be a bridge monkey."

"What's that?" you ask.

"They're the workers who build the trestles and bridges that cross over gullies and ravines," he says. "They usually work about 20 miles or so ahead of the tracklayers."

"Finally, there are the roustabouts," he continues. "They work on grading the roadbed, smoothing out hills, and filling in holes with dirt and stone. They are far ahead of the track construction, 200 miles or more out on the prairie."

They're all challenging jobs. But none are too hard for you.

To be a tracklayer, turn to page 44.

To be a bridge monkey, turn to page 46.

To be a roustabout, turn to page 51.

You arrive at the end of the railroad line near the tent town of Julesburg, Nebraska. You are immediately assigned to a gang of workers, all of them Irish.

"Welcome to the team, Tarrier," the gang leader, Sean, says. Later you learn the name comes from people's calling Irish workers "terriers," because you are as tough as terrier dogs. But the Irish accent makes the word sound like "tarrier," and the nickname stuck. You even sing a song about yourselves as you work, "Drill, Ye Tarriers, Drill!"

Your gang lifts each 500-pound rail off a boxcar and carries it to the railroad tie. You lay it in place and then the spikers hammer in ten spikes to secure it. Then it's on to the next rail. On your first day you lay down a mile of rail, an average day's work on the flat plains.

The long workday is over. The other
men in your gang are heading into town to
enjoy themselves.

"Come along," says Sean. "We'll have a good
time." You've heard good and bad things about
nearby Julesburg. It's not really a town, just another
of the temporary places that have sprouted up
along the railroad line. The people who gather
there are looking to do business with the railroad
workers. They include tavern owners, card players,
tricksters, and outlaws out to steal your money.

"Are you coming or not?" Sean persists. You're
bone tired, but you think it might be fun to see the
town with your new friends.

45

To go into town, turn to page 47.

To stay in camp, turn to page 52.

You have a talent for building and know a few things about carpentry. Working on bridges suits you just fine.

The first bridge you are assigned to is already under construction. It is very tall, and crosses a gap in the land several hundred feet wide. Men are needed on the ground to build the supports for the bridge. Others are working up on top where the wooden railroad ties are being put in place.

Railroad workers slept and ate their meals in tight quarters inside train cars.

46

To work on the ground, turn to page 48.

To work up above, turn to page 49.

Julesberg has a reputation as "The Wickedest City in the West." Feeling cautious, you try to stay alert as you head into town.

Every other building you pass is a saloon or gambling hall. You hear the sounds of piano music, singing dance hall girls, and the rough laughter of men. Your bunch enters a gambling place where a group of men are sitting at a table playing poker.

A black-vested man looks up from his cards. "We've got room for one more," he says. "Would one of you gentlemen care to join us?"

Sean nudges you. "Go on, didn't you tell me you were a good poker player?" he says.

That's true. You could probably win a few hands. Still, it might be wiser to save your money for a good steak dinner.

To join the poker game, turn to page 68.

To look for food, turn to page 56.

You decide the conditions above look too risky so you choose to work down below.

You lift the heavy wooden beams with your work team and hammer them in place. It is exhausting work.

When it's finally break time you are grateful for the rest. After only a few minutes the foreman taps you on the shoulder. He needs men to lift some timber from a nearby pile to be hauled up by rope to the men working on the tracks.

Turn to page 65.

You climb up the trestle to the top of the bridge. You have no problem working here with the other men, as long as you don't look down. It's a long drop to the valley below. But the view of the sky above is grand. It fills you with energy.

Another Irishman, Mick, is working alongside you. You talk about what you are going to do with the money you earn when the railroad is finished. Mick plans to bring his family west and start a farm. You have no family yet, but want to visit San Francisco and maybe settle there.

As you talk and work, Mick's hammer slips from his hand and falls on a lower board on the trestle. He reaches for it and slips. Suddenly he is hanging by his hands from the trestle.

"Help!" he cries.

49

Turn the page.

You want to help him, but the edge of the trestle may not hold your weight. Then you'll both fall to your deaths. There's a rope nearby. You could toss it to Mick and pull him up.

Railway bridges had to be built quickly to keep the construction on schedule.

50

To go rescue him yourself, turn to page 60.

To throw Mick the rope, turn to page 64.

You travel by horse-drawn wagon to the edge of Wyoming Territory. The home of the Sioux and other American Indian tribes is just to the northwest.

The railroad is cutting through land the Indians have hunted on for generations, and they don't like it. The government has not kept its promise of respecting Indian territory.

It takes you and the other new recruits days to reach the prairie, which is more than 100 miles beyond Julesburg. You arrive at a rocky site where workers are filling in a wide ravine with earth and stone.

Turn to page 53.

You decide to stay behind and head for dinner. Everything in camp is in the work train, as it's called. Each railroad car serves a purpose—supplies, tools, food, and sleeping accommodations. You enter the dining car and sit down at a long table with 125 other hungry men. You eat off tin plates. The plates are nailed down to the table so they can be washed right there, saving the servers time.

After eating, you head for a sleeping boxcar. Bunks and hammocks are filled with tired men. You notice one man, Hiram, leaving with his bedding.

"Where are you going?" you ask him.

"I'm sleeping outside in a tent," Hiram says. "It's better than putting up with the rats and bedbugs in this place."

Maybe Hiram has a good idea.

To sleep outside, turn to page 55.

To sleep in the boxcar, turn to page 59.

One morning you are filling carts with earth and stone to dump down into the ravine. A mule pulls the cart to the edge. It is the only time you get a brief break from your labor. The hot midday sun beats down. Your tanned skin has turned a deep brown.

You look up to see clouds of dust in the distance. A few moments later you can make out a war party of Sioux on horseback, racing straight for your crew. You remember your rifle is about a hundred yards away in your tent. Can you reach it before the Sioux bear down on you? Or should you leap into the ravine and hide?

To run for your rifle, turn to page 54.

To jump into the ravine and hide, turn to page 66.

You race for the tents. Other men are running there too, with the same thought in mind—get a rifle. You're almost there—when you feel a sharp pang in your shoulder. Then there's another searing stab in your left leg. You drop to the ground, two arrows protruding from your body.

You hear the horse hooves growing closer and the cries of warriors and the men of your crew. Your first instinct is to crawl for the tent and get that rifle. But what if another Sioux spots you? Instead, you could play dead and hope they don't discover you're still alive.

54

To play dead, turn to page 57.

To crawl to the tent, turn to page 67.

You help Hiram pitch a tent outside. Several other sleepy men join you. Someone has built a small fire to provide some warmth on this cold night.

You settle down and soon drift off to sleep. All at once, you are awakened by a rumbling noise. It grows increasingly louder.

You think it's one of those sudden lightning storms that roll without warning across the Great Plains. But it's not.

"Buffalo," cries Hiram. "Run for your lives!"

In the dying flames of the fire you can make out the massive buffalo herd bearing down on you. You can run for the boxcars. Or you can go for the rail tracks. It's possible the stampeding buffalo will avoid going over the tracks. But you can't be sure.

55

To run for the tracks, turn to page 58.

To go for the boxcars, turn to page 61.

"Who's hungry?" you say to your friends, leading the way out of the gambling hall.

You find a place to eat down the street. The steak you order tastes much better than the buffalo meat served back in the dining car. After eating you walk around town a bit. A fight has broken out in the gambling hall you visited earlier. You're glad you're not part of the proceedings. Soon you head back to camp. You're tired and ready for bed.

56

As railroad workers built westward, businesses such as saloons and other stores opened along the route.

Turn to page 59.

You lie perfectly still. War whoops, rifle fire, and the cries of the men on your crew assault your ears. You squeeze your eyes tight and wish you could shut your ears as well. You hear footsteps drawing near.

A foot prods your side. The person is wearing a moccasin and you know he is a Sioux. You don't breathe or move a muscle. All at once, you feel a hand grip your hair. This is followed by a searing pain on the top of your head. You grit your teeth to stop yourself from crying out. You realize your scalp is being cut off your head with all your hair.

Turn to page 62.

You run for the railroad tracks. They're closer and perhaps the stampeding buffalo will avoid them. You fling yourself down on the track bed. Buffalo have been known to run over the rails, but this time their path takes a different direction. The sound of the stampeding animals recedes into the distance. You rise to your feet, shaken, but very much alive.

You decide you'll sleep in the boxcar for the rest of the night. You'd rather deal with rats and bugs than another herd of stampeding buffalo.

Go to page 59.

You enjoy a good night's sleep in the boxcar. Days and weeks pass. You continue to lay track across the Plains.

You cross through Wyoming Territory. The months have turned into years, and now, as you near Utah Territory, home of the Mormons, you hear that the Central Pacific and the Union Pacific will soon meet. They will come together at a place called Promontory Summit. You and your fellow Tarriers look forward to that day. All the work you have done these past few years will come to a glorious end. The transcontinental railroad will be completed, a nation united, and you will have played your part in this great accomplishment.

THE END

To follow another path, turn to page 11.
To read the conclusion, turn to page 101.

Risking your own life, you crawl out on the beams to try to save Mick. You reach the edge of the bridge where he hangs.

"Give me your hand," you say, reaching out.

He does, and you pull with all your strength. Inch by inch, Mick rises from the edge and finally flops down on the bridge, huffing and puffing.

"Thanks, laddie," he says, grasping your shoulder.

The men below are yelling, "Hooray!" You are the hero of the day. Now it's back to work on the transcontinental railroad.

60

THE END

To follow another path, turn to page 11.
To read the conclusion, turn to page 101.

You get to your feet and begin to run for the boxcars. You hear other men running alongside you in the pitch dark. Somebody bumps up against you and you fall to the hard earth. You get up, stumble on a root and fall again.

The thundering hoofbeats grow louder. You rise to your feet, but it is too late. There's no time to outrun the herd of buffalo that descends on you. Your body is crushed under the pounding hooves of these massive creatures, and you gasp for your last breath.

THE END

To follow another path, turn to page 11.
To read the conclusion, turn to page 101.

The warrior has finished his gruesome task. You hear him move away, to look for more scalps to take as war trophies.

Attacks on the railway workers by American Indians were not uncommon. The railroad cut through Indian land, and some tribes considered this an act of war. They aimed to disrupt the railroad's progress using any method they could.

Your head is bleeding and you want to scream, but you don't dare. Five minutes pass. It seems like five hours. You hear hoofbeats receding into the distance. You open your eyes and look around at the scattered bodies of your friends. You alone have survived the attack. You stumble to your feet and manage to climb onto a horse. You ride 10 miles to the next roustabout camp. You tell the crew your grim tale. A doctor treats your arrow wounds and cleans and bandages your throbbing head.

Eventually your wounds heal. You return to work and find that your amazing survival story has become well known. You stick with the job until the railroad is complete, bearing terrible scars but happy to be alive with a unique story to tell.

THE END

To follow another path, turn to page 11.
To read the conclusion, turn to page 101.

You grab the rope and toss one end to Mick. He grabs it and you start to pull. The rope is old and frayed. It starts to tear apart at the point where it meets the board.

You pull faster and call out for help from the other men. But before they can reach you, the rope splits. With a terrible cry, Mick falls.

You gaze down at his still body far below. Men are gathering around it. If only you had tried to rescue him without the rope, he might be alive. Mick's death causes you great distress. The next day you quit your job and head east. You are through working for the railroad.

THE END

To follow another path, turn to page 11.
To read the conclusion, turn to page 101.

You and three other men head for the pile of timber. You reach down into the pile and hear a loud hissing sound. Suddenly a rattlesnake lunges out and bites your leg. One of the other crew members pulls out a pistol and shoots the snake dead. The men help you back to the main camp.

The foreman has some experience with snakebites. He takes a knife and cuts a cross over your bite. He puts his mouth to the wound and sucks out the snake venom. But he doesn't get all of it.

The wound festers and the leg turns gangrenous. A railroad doctor decides to amputate to save your life. You lose your leg and your job on the railroad.

65

THE END

To follow another path, turn to page 11.
To read the conclusion, turn to page 101.

You leap into the ravine and land in a heap. You get to your feet, aching all over, and look up to see a Sioux warrior glaring down at you. He holds a rifle in his hands. He fires and misses you by inches. Before he can fire again, you pick up a rock and hurl it at him. You hit him on the head and he loses his footing and tumbles into the ravine.

The Sioux is knocked out in the fall and you take the rifle from his hands. You climb out of the ravine and join the other roustabouts in driving off the attackers. They may attack again, but next time you'll be ready for them. From now on, your gun will always be by your side. You stick with the job until the railroad is complete. Years later you tell your grandchildren about the dangers you survived while working for the Union Pacific.

THE END

To follow another path, turn to page 11.
To read the conclusion, turn to page 101.

You start to crawl, inch by inch. You hear a horse drawing near. You stop and lie still. But it is too late. A keen-eyed warrior has spotted you moving. You look up and see him on horseback. He lifts the sharp lance in his hand and plunges it into your chest. Your death is mercifully swift.

The Pawnee Indian tribe welcomed the Union Pacific. They were given free passage on the railroad and were hired as scouts. A group of Pawnee warriors even patrolled the railroad to protect workers from Sioux raiders.

THE END

To follow another path, turn to page 11.
To read the conclusion, turn to page 101.

"I'm in," you say and take a seat. Sean and your other friends watch. The man in the vest shuffles the cards and deals. You can tell from the way he deals that he is a professional gambler. You decide to keep a close eye on him.

The game moves quickly. As the gambler studies his cards he tugs at his shirtsleeve and you think you see a card slip out from his sleeve.

You present your hand and he shows his. He beats you with two aces and two kings. He starts to draw in his winnings when you put a hand on his wrist.

"Hold on," you say. "I think there's something wrong here."

The gambler's eyes narrow on you. "Are you calling me a cheat?" he asks.

The gambler reaches in his vest and pulls out a tiny pistol called a derringer. You grab for your gun. He fires first and his bullet grazes your shoulder. You fire and the derringer flies out of the gambler's hand.

The town sheriff walks through the gathered crowd. He puts you both under arrest for disturbing the peace. You spend the night in jail, and pay a fine the next morning.

But there's more bad news. Word of your little gunfight got back to camp, and the foreman fires you for being a troublemaker. Now you're low on money, out of a job, and stuck in a town you want nothing more to do with.

THE END

To follow another path, turn to page 11.
To read the conclusion, turn to page 101.

A steam shovel crew makes improvements to the rail line in 1869.

CHAPTER 4

RACE TO THE FINISH

It is early April 1869. For more than six long years the Union Pacific and the Central Pacific have worked their way across half a continent to complete the transcontinental railroad. Now their work is drawing to an end.

You are a young, hard-working engineer on the Central Pacific. Your boss is construction supervisor Charles Crocker, one of the Central Pacific's owners. One day Crocker calls you into his office.

71

Turn the page.

"I've just received word that a place has been chosen for the two railroads to meet," Crocker tells you. "It's a spot called Promontory Summit in Utah, just north of the Great Salt Lake.

"We've got to beat the Union Pacific to Promontory," he tells you. "We'll show those Easterners who's better at laying tracks!"

Crocker's enthusiasm catches fire with you. You're ready to do whatever it takes to make the Central Pacific number one. But what job will you fill? Crocker has already thought about this.

"You're a fine engineer and a young man I have the highest trust in," he tells you.

"There are three tasks I need a good man for and I'll let you pick the one you want," Crocker explains.

The first job is helping him oversee the Chinese construction crews in the last drive to Promontory Summit. The second is checking out the rumors of tension between the Chinese and the Irish of the Union Pacific on the advanced grading crews. If it's true, someone will have to put an end to the trouble before fighting breaks out. Finally, someone is needed to pick up the golden spike that will be used as a symbol in the final ceremony. It must be delivered to Central Pacific owner Leland Stanford.

To work with the construction crews, turn to page 74.

To check out the troubles on the advance crews, turn to page 76.

To get the golden spike, turn to page 82.

Charlie Crocker puts you to work supervising the final stretch of track laying. After he hears that a Union Pacific crew managed to lay more than 8 miles of track in one day, he decides to do better.

He declares April 28th "Ten Mile Day." Together you pick the best Chinese tracklayers and offer them four days' wages for one long day's work. Will they be able to lay 10 miles of track in a single day and set a record? Time will tell.

Early on the morning of April 28th, dozens of newspaper reporters, photographers, and curiosity seekers gather at the rail side to watch this feat. A train whistle screeches. It's the signal for the men to go to work.

Sixteen railroad cars filled with iron rails are unloaded by the work site. Eight burly Irishmen lift each 30-foot-long, 560-pound rail and set it in place. Then the Chinese construction crew lays the ties and secures them with spikes.

By noon they have laid 6 miles of track and earned a break for lunch. You walk among the workers with words of praise and encouragement.

The afternoon gets off to a fast start, but some of the men are beginning to tire. One Irishman is struggling to lift the heavy rail with his gang. You could take his place for a while and give him a chance to regain his strength. Or you could push him to keep going. Either way, the work can't stop.

To take the worker's place, turn to page 77.
To push him to keep working, turn to page 96.

You head to a work site near Promontory Summit. Rival crews of the Union Pacific and your own Central Pacific are working within 100 feet of one another, grading the roadway for the tracks.

As you talk to Hank, a foreman for the Chinese crews, a Union Pacific Irishman throws a frozen ball of earth at one of the Chinese workers and hits him in the head. Other Chinese workers yell angrily and shake their fists. A fight is brewing.

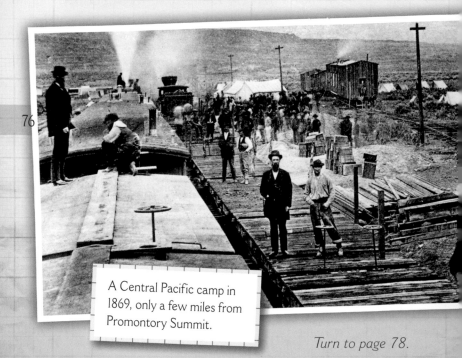

A Central Pacific camp in 1869, only a few miles from Promontory Summit.

Turn to page 78.

"Take a break," you say to the tired Irishman. "Come back when you're rested."

He's so weary that he doesn't protest. He just nods gratefully and wanders off.

You take his place on the rail gang. You quickly feel your muscles aching from lifting the rails, but it feels good to be doing physical labor for a change. You feel a part of things in a way you never felt before. Still, when the Irishman returns a half hour later, you're just as relieved to turn the work over to him.

The hours fly by. Just before 7:00 p.m. a foreman comes up to Crocker and whispers something in his ear. Crocker smiles and calls the workday to a halt and asks the men to gather around.

Turn to page 98.

The Chinese and Irish workers begin hurling insults at one another. The tension is mounting. Some of the Union Pacific Irishmen are rolling up their sleeves, ready to fight.

You start to move to stop the impending violence. But Hank puts a hand on your shoulder. "Let them fight for a while," he says. "They need to blow off some steam. They'll stop in a bit. If you get involved, it will only get worse."

You're not sure you agree with Hank, but maybe he's right.

78

To try to stop them, go to page 79.

To let the men fight, turn to page 97.

You gather together a group of foremen and meet the Irish Union Pacific workers before they reach the Chinese.

"You men are here to work, not fight," you tell them. "Now get back to your own work site."

A big Irishman with a red beard steps forward. "You're not our boss," he says. "We don't take orders from the Central Pacific."

The other Irishmen mutter their approval.

"That's true," you reply, "but these workers you're attacking do work for me, and I won't have you hurting them."

An ugly grin spreads across the big man's face. "So what do you intend to do about it, Mr. Engineer?"

79

Turn the page.

You see the men starting to circle around you. One of your foremen reaches for the gun in his belt. You stop him.

"Listen to me," you say to the Union Pacific workers. "We're close to the finish. Every mile of track you lay brings us closer to Promontory and puts more money in your pocket. So why waste time fighting each other?"

The big man with the red beard stares sullenly at you, but the other men start to back away. Your words make sense to them. Finally, begrudgingly, the big man follows them.

You breathe a sigh of relief, knowing this could have ended very differently.

The next day you are called to Crocker's office. Word of your bold actions has reached his ears. He tells you he needs a man with your courage and determination to go to San Francisco and get the golden spike and bring it to Leland Stanford.

Crocker is counting on you. You accept the job.

April 28, 1869, became famous as the day Central Pacific crews built more than 10 miles of track in just under 12 hours. Chinese laborers joined Irish workers to make this feat possible.

Turn to page 82.

You travel to San Francisco to pick up the golden spike from the foundry where it was made. William T. Garatt, the foundry owner, shows it to you. "It's made of 17.6 carat gold," he tells you, placing it in a small, specially made box. "Guard it with your life."

Your next stop is Sacramento, California's capital. There you will hand over the golden spike to former governor Leland Stanford, another member of the Big Four. He will take it to Promontory Summit for the closing ceremony on May 8. You prepare to board a stagecoach for Sacramento.

Just before boarding the stagecoach, you tuck the golden spike in your coat pocket. It is crowded inside the coach. On one side of you sits a young woman. On the other side is a small man wearing a derby hat. You settle in to enjoy the trip.

After several hours the driver brings the stagecoach to an abrupt stop. You look out the window and see that two men, brandishing guns, have stopped the stagecoach. It's a holdup!

One of the men orders you and the other passengers out of the stagecoach. At gunpoint he asks each of you to empty your pockets and place your valuables into his hat.

Robbers usually found remote spots where stagecoaches had to slow down, then approached with guns drawn.

To give up the golden spike, turn to page 84.
To refuse to empty your pockets, turn to page 86.

You hand the outlaw your wallet, but don't empty your coat pockets.

"Keep going," he says, poking his gun in your face. "You're not finished."

Reluctantly, you hand over the small box in your coat pocket. The man opens it, sees the golden spike, and gives a loud whistle.

Before he can examine the spike more closely, the little man in the derby is holding a gun to the robber's head.

"Let's drop that and the gun, too, friend," he says. You stare at him, as stunned as the robber is.

The other robber fires a shot, but he misses the man, who then shoots the gun from the robber's hand. He then ties up the two crooks with you and the stagecoach driver helping.

"I'll stay here with them," the little man tells the driver. "You go into town and let the marshal know we're here. I'm sure he has a jail cell that can accommodate these two gentlemen."

"I never would have taken you for a lawman," you say to the little man.

"I'm no lawman," he replies. "I work for the Pinkerton Detective Agency. The stagecoach line hired us to go undercover and investigate the robberies they've been having. Have a pleasant ride to Sacramento."

Turn to page 87.

You shake your head.

"Are you itching to get shot?" the outlaw says.

"Don't be a fool," the young woman says to you.

The outlaw smiles at the woman, turning his head to look at her. In that moment, you make your move. You grab his hand and twist his wrist. He drops the gun.

The other robber fires, and you feel the bullet pierce your shoulder. The stagecoach driver grabs his rifle. The robbers run for their horses and ride off, the driver firing at them.

The driver thanks you for your courage. The money shipment on board has been saved, as well as the golden spike.

Your fellow passengers congratulate you, while several of them tend to your wounded shoulder. You are a hero.

Go to page 87.

After your arrival in Sacramento Stanford is busy preparing for the trip to Promontory Summit on a special train. He is happy to see you and receive the golden spike.

"You've come this far," he says. "Why not travel with me and my guests to Promontory Summit?"

You are flattered by his offer and accept. You will represent the Central Pacific's engineers at the final ceremony on May 8.

Stanford's train has only two cars. In one Stanford and his guests will eat and sleep. The other is filled with delicious food for the trip and the stay in Utah. It includes everything from live chickens to case after case of champagne.

On May 5 the train leaves the Sacramento station for the 690-mile journey to Promontory Summit.

Turn to page 88.

Soon after the train crosses into Utah it comes to a screeching halt.

"What's the meaning of this?" Stanford demands of the train's conductor.

"This bridge ahead of us doesn't look all that sturdy," the conductor explains. "I think someone should inspect it to make sure it's safe to cross."

Some wooden trestle bridges were rickety enough that trains had to move very slowly to cross safely.

You share the conductor's concern. You know that many of the bridges on the transcontinental railroad, especially those built in the last few months, have been slapped together hastily to keep the work on schedule. Many of them will have to be rebuilt later.

Stanford, however, wants to stay on schedule to get to the ceremony on time. He turns to you, the only engineer on board. "What do you think?" he asks. "Is that bridge safe enough or do you need to inspect it first?"

You think hard before you answer. The train conductor could be right. Or maybe the bridge is secure enough to take the weight of your small train. Stanford obviously doesn't want to waste time with an inspection.

To make the inspection, turn to page 90.

To skip the inspection, turn to page 91.

"I think it would be wise to make an inspection of the bridge, Governor," you say.

Stanford isn't pleased to hear this, but he defers to your expertise. "Just make it as quick as you can," he tells you.

You ask the conductor to make the inspection with you. You walk along the bridge tracks. They are not the most secure, but seem strong enough to hold the small train. The conductor agrees with you.

Shortly after, he starts up the train and you begin to cross the bridge. The tracks shake and rattle, but you assure everyone that they will hold. You are relieved when the train finishes crossing safely.

The following day you arrive at Promontory Summit only to find out that the train carrying Dr. Durant of the Union Pacific has been delayed. The ceremony has been postponed until May 10.

Turn to page 92.

90

You tell Stanford that you don't think an inspection is necessary. This is just what he wanted to hear. The driver starts up the train and it slowly goes onto the bridge. The tracks rattle, and the train shakes. Guests on board gasp and hold their breath. You feel sick to your stomach, wishing you could say something to reassure the passengers. But since you didn't make an inspection you have no idea whether the tracks will hold or not.

The train, however, makes it safely to the other side.

"That bridge is about to collapse," Stanford mutters to you. "What kind of engineers do I have that would approve such a bridge as safe?"

Turn to page 99.

Promontory Summit is a tent city, not much different than the other temporary towns that sprouted up along the railroad line. The morning of May 10 is cloudy and cold. By noon the tracks are mobbed with people. The Central Pacific's *Jupiter* locomotive and the Union Pacific's more humble *Engine Number 119* are separated by only one unfinished railroad tie.

Men have placed the golden spike and three other ceremonial spikes into pre-bored holes in a tie made of laurel wood. Leland Stanford taps the golden spike gently in place in the hole. As the politicians make speeches and the local bands play music, workmen remove the four ceremonial spikes and laurel tie. They replace them with a pine tie and iron spikes to be placed on the tracks.

Governor Stanford and Dr. Durant step onto the tracks. The two men are bitter rivals, but this morning they greet each other with smiles.

The hammer to be used on the last spike has been attached to a telegraph wire. When it strikes the spike, a message will automatically be sent across the nation: the transcontinental railroad is completed.

Governor Stanford takes the hammer first. He swings it down on the spike … and misses! You hear some of the railroad workers snickering. The great railroad executive can't even hit a spike with a hammer!

93

Turn the page.

urant takes the hammer from Stanford
wings it. He, too, misses the spike! The
ghter from the crowd grows louder. Both men
are red with embarrassment. Someone should
do something to save this historic moment from
becoming a complete disaster. You decide that
person will be you.

Two locomotives were brought face to face as the two tracks were connected.

You spot a railroad worker with big hands standing nearby. You lean over and whisper something in his ear.

He nods and steps between the two powerful men. He takes the hammer from Durant. Then he expertly pounds the spike into the tie. The crowd cheers. The telegraph operator has already sent the message out on the telegraph—three dots that say the job is done.

Stanford and Durant regain their composure and shake hands. "There is henceforth but one Pacific Railroad in the United States," cries Durant as the crowd cheers again.

The race is over. The transcontinental railroad is finished. And you are proud to have done your part to make this historic occasion a success.

THE END

To follow another path, turn to page 11.
To read the conclusion, turn to page 101.

"Come on, man," you say to the Irishman. "Let's not fall down on the job!"

But a few minutes later, that's exactly what the poor fellow does. His grip slips on the rail he is holding and the other lifters lose their balance. The rail drops to the ground—right on your foot.

You cry out in pain, and the men manage to lift the rail off your foot. Several of them help you to a tent, where a doctor examines you. Your foot appears to be broken in several places. The doctor orders you to stay off of your feet for the next few weeks. Crocker finds another man to oversee the track laying. You have no choice but to stay behind, resting your injured foot.

96

THE END

To follow another path, turn to page 11.
To read the conclusion, turn to page 101.

The verbal insults between the Irish and Chinese turn into an all-out brawl. Fistfights break out up and down the rail line. You watch and do nothing to stop it. Then you see some of the Irish swing pickaxes at your Chinese workers.

You run into the middle of the fighters and order them to stop at once. No one pays any attention. You look down and see two Chinese workers bleeding and groaning in pain.

Suddenly there is a loud explosion. In revenge, the Chinese have set off dynamite charges without warning the Union Pacific workers. Two of the Irishmen lie still on the ground. You feel sick. You have allowed this tragedy to happen. You resign out of shame and fear of what Charlie Crocker will say when he hears about the incident.

THE END

To follow another path, turn to page 11.
To read the conclusion, turn to page 101.

"Gentlemen," Crocker announces, "you have just laid 10 miles and 56 feet of track since this morning. That's a one-day record!"

The workers give a loud cheer. The Ten Mile Day has lived up to its name.

"Let's see the Union Pacific beat that record," you say to Crocker. He gives a deep laugh.

"My boy," he says, "they couldn't beat it no matter how hard they tried. You see, they have only 9 miles of track left to lay between where they are now and Promontory Summit!" You both have a good laugh over that. You smile, happy to have helped build this great railroad that will soon connect the country.

THE END

To follow another path, turn to page 11.
To read the conclusion, turn to page 101.

You want to tell Stanford that he himself gave the orders to build quickly to keep up the pace of construction, but you don't want to make him any angrier.

When the train arrives in Promontory Summit, one of Stanford's aides informs you that you have been let go from your position. So ends your great adventure on the transcontinental railroad.

THE END

To follow another path, turn to page 11.
To read the conclusion, turn to page 101.

The new railroad boasted luxurious cars for wealthy passengers.

CHAPTER 5

A NATION UNITED

The completion of the first transcontinental railroad was a major landmark in American history. It was also one of the great engineering feats of the 1800s.

Before the railroad was built, it took people months to travel from one end of the country to the other. Now, by train, it took only a week. The journey was safe, clean, and comfortable. It was inexpensive enough to accommodate middle and lower income Americans as well as foreign immigrants from Europe. Hundreds of thousands of Americans headed west to settle land and start new lives.

The vast regions of the Great Plains were settled by people looking for fertile land for farming. Farms, new towns, and cities began to spring up in the West.

Accommodations for lower class passengers could be very uncomfortable.

Many towns, such as Julesburg, Nebraska, sprang up alongside the railroad. A few of them survived and grew into permanent communities. Among these was Cheyenne, which became the capital of Wyoming in 1890.

Even before the Union Pacific and the Central Pacific met at Promontory Summit, other railroad companies were working on their own transcontinental lines. Within a generation, four new railroads spanned the nation—the Northern Pacific, the Southern Pacific, the Santa Fe, and the Great Northern. Stanford and Huntington and the other railroad leaders were joined by new railroad tycoons who built these railroads and became rich as a result.

A Central Pacific train passing through a Nevada canyon in 1869.

The true unsung heroes of the transcontinental railroad were the thousands of workers. They built the railroad with muscle, courage, and pure grit. Some of them died on the job—by blasts of explosives or terrible falls. Their memories and achievements live on in ballads and songs, stories and folklore.

The transcontinental railroad was also a symbol of unity. After the terrible Civil War that divided the United States so dramatically, the transcontinental railroad represented a step toward bringing the country together again—physically and spiritually. It became the vital link that helped to settle the West, bring goods and services wherever they were needed, and make the nation whole again.

TIMELINE

1830—The *Tom Thumb*, the first American-built steam locomotive, is tested on a railroad track between Baltimore and Ellicott's Mills in Maryland.

April 12, 1861—A Southern attack on federal troops at Fort Sumter, South Carolina, signals the start of the Civil War.

October 1861—Engineer Theodore Judah comes to Washington to advocate for a reasonable route westward for a transcontinental railroad.

July 1, 1862—President Abraham Lincoln signs the Pacific Railroad Act, promoting the construction of the transcontinental railroad.

January 8, 1863—California Governor Leland Stanford officiates at the groundbreaking ceremony for the Central Pacific Railroad in Sacramento.

December 2, 1863—The Union Pacific breaks ground at Omaha, Nebraska; however, financial problems delay the start of construction by nearly a year.

April 9, 1865—The Civil War ends with General Robert E. Lee's surrender at Appomattox, Virginia, paving the way for the transcontinental railroad to go forward.

January 1865—The Central Pacific hires its first group of Chinese laborers. Within a few years, thousands of Chinese are working on the railroad.

1866–1867—Snow and ice in one of the worst winters on record in the Sierra Nevada nearly brings work on the railroad to a standstill.

June 25, 1867—Two thousand Chinese workers go on strike, demanding $40 a month in pay and a 10-hour workday. The strike fails and in a week they return to work.

August 28, 1867—Central Pacific workers finally break through the rock of the Summit Tunnel, the most difficult of many challenging tunnel projects in the Sierra Nevada.

April 28, 1869—Central Pacific crews meet the challenge of laying 10 miles of rail in one day.

May 10, 1869—In a day of celebration, the final rail and spike are put in place at Promontory Summit, Utah, completing the transcontinental railroad.

OTHER PATHS TO EXPLORE

In this book, you've seen how events from the past look different from three points of view. Perspectives on history are as varied as the people who lived it. Seeing history from many points of view is an important part of understanding it. Here are ideas for other transcontinental railroad points of view to explore:

+ Some American Indian tribes saw the railroad as a threat and tried to stop it. They tore up tracks, attacked work crews, and later attacked trains and passengers. Why do you think the American Indians were so opposed to the railroad, and was their reaction justified? Support your answer with examples from the text and other sources. (Integration of Knowledge and Ideas)

+ The railroad owners were motivated more by greed than public service. Yet their energy and business savvy helped to create the transcontinental railroad. Do the ends justify the means in this case? Can American businessmen and women, even today, be less competitive and more ethical and still succeed? Explain why or why not. Support your answer with examples from the text and other sources. (Integration of Knowledge and Ideas)

READ MORE

Durbin, William. *Until the Last Spike: The Journal of Sean Sullivan, a Transcontinental Railroad Worker, Nebraska and Points West, 1867.* My Name Is America. New York: Scholastic, 2013.

Perritano, John. *The Transcontinental Railroad.* New York: Children's Press, 2010.

Santella, Andrew. *Plains Indians.* Chicago: Heinemann Library, 2012.

INTERNET SITES

FactHound offers a safe, fun way to find Internet sites related to this book. All of the sites on FactHound have been researched by our staff.

Here's all you do:

Visit *www.facthound.com*

Type in this code: 9781491404010

GLOSSARY

derringer (DER-in-juhr)—a short-barreled pocket pistol

immigrant (IM-uh-gruhnt)—a person who moves from one country to live permanently in another

isthmus (ISS-muhss)—a narrow strip of land that has water on both sides and connects two larger sections of land

locomotive (loh-kuh-MOH-tiv)—an engine used to push or pull railroad cars

nitroglycerine (nye-troh-GLISS-uhr-in)—an explosive liquid used to make very powerful explosions

queue (KYOO)—a braid of hair that hangs down behind the head, once worn by Chinese men

roustabout (ROUST-uh-bout)—an unskilled laborer

transcontinental (transs-kon-tuh-NEN-tuhl)—having to do with extending or going across a continent

venom (VEN-uhm)—a poisonous liquid produced by some animals

BIBLIOGRAPHY

Ambrose, Stephen E. *Nothing Like It In the World: The Men Who Built the Transcontinental Railroad 1863-1869.* New York: Simon & Schuster, 2000.

Bain, David Haward. *Empire Express: Building the First Transcontinental Railroad.* New York: Viking, 1999.

Blumberg, Rhoda. *Full Steam Ahead: The Race to Build a Transcontinental Railroad.* Washington D.C.: National Geographic Society, 1996.

Cadbury, Deborah. *Dreams of Iron and Steel: Seven Wonders of the Nineteenth Century, from the Building of the London Sewers to the Panama Canal.* New York: Fourth Estate, 2004.

History: *Transcontinental Railroad.* 29 April, 2014. http://www.history.com/topics/inventions/transcontinental-railroad.

Library of Congress: History of Railroads and Maps. 29 April, 2014. http://memory.loc.gov/ammem/gmdhtml/rrhtml/rrintro.html.

PBS: *Transcontinental Railroad.* 29 April, 2014. http://www.pbs.org/wgbh/americanexperience/films/tcrr/.

Wheeler, Keith. *The Railroaders.* New York: Time-Life Books, 1973.

INDEX